THE BEST OF
THAILAND
A COOKBOOK

Evie Righter, Series Editor

Recipes by Grace Young
Food Photography by Steven Mark Needham

CollinsPublishersSanFrancisco
A Division of HarperCollinsPublishers

First published in USA 1993 by Collins Publishers San Francisco
1160 Battery Street, San Francisco, CA 94111

Produced by Smallwood and Stewart Inc.,
New York City

© 1993 Smallwood and Stewart, Inc.

Edited by Kimberly Horstman
Jacket design by Carol Bokuniewicz
Food styling by Sandra Robishaw
Prop styling by Bette Blau

Photography credits: Jeffrey Alford/Asia Access: 1; 21.
Luca Invernizzi Tettoni/Photobank: 2–3; 12; 17; 39; 75; 83. Robert
Harding/Picture Perfect: 7; 53. Jean-Jacques/Picture Perfect: 55.
Prop credits: All antique baskets and wooden plates from Beseated Inc.

Library of Congress Cataloging-in-Publication Data

Righter, Evie
    The best of Thailand : a cookbook / Evie Righter ;
recipes by Grace Young ; food photography by Steven
Mark Needham.
        p.   cm.
    Includes index.
    ISBN 0-00-255206-X: $14.95
    1. Cookery, Thai.   I. Title.
TX724.5.T5R54   1993
641.59593—dc20
                                                    92-37715
                                                    CIP

Printed in Hong Kong

Contents

Introduction

"Exotic" perfectly describes Thailand, once known as Siam. As the only Southeast Asian country never to have been colonized by the West, Thailand has always had an enchanting, mysterious aura. Although culturally influenced by both China and India and surrounded by turbulent neighbors such as Laos, Vietnam, and Cambodia, a benevolent, enlightened monarchy that lasted centuries allowed the peace-loving Thais to evolve in very much their own way.

It is not surprising that the Thais are passionate about food: With long growing seasons and a stable environment, the country yields an abundance of marvelous ingredients for the kitchen. Its vast, fertile plains in the north invite massive cultivation of rice, the most important element in the Thai diet. Miles of coastline on both the Indian Ocean and the Gulf of Thailand provide an endless variety of seafood and shellfish. Thailand is also blessed with a wealth of fruits, many of which ~ rambutans, durians, and mangosteens, for example ~ are almost unknown in the West even today.

What is the cooking of Thailand? With a healthy pinch of Chinese influence in the preparation of certain foods, and a generous dash of

Ko Pipi Island in the Andaman Sea

Indian influence in the use of spices and the making of curries, Thai food is uniquely its own. It is of two minds: It can be sweet and soothing, or hot and spicy almost beyond imagination. As in Chinese cooking, it has a subtle balance of sweet, salty, and sour flavors that creates harmony through contrast, completeness through the sum of their dissimilar parts. And it always employs the freshest ingredients, whether they are bought at Bangkok's unique floating market or at a local farmers' market.

The Thai pantry includes several important ingredients: *nam pla*, or fish sauce, which lends saltiness to a dish; fresh chili peppers; and herbs, among them the fragrant lemongrass, coriander root, galangal (a relative of gingerroot), and tamarind pulp, which when soaked gives forth an assertive, sour juice. Spicy pastes figure importantly in the cooking of Thailand. Among the most popular are red curry paste, based on dried chili peppers; green curry paste, potent with fresh green chilis; and Masaman curry paste, with dried red chili peppers and a host of spices from the Indian spice routes. Coconut milk is a staple in Thailand, serving as the base of sauces, soups, vegetable dishes, and desserts. Seafood is the favorite main dish, but when it is not available (as in inland areas), chicken, pork, and beef are popular alternatives.

The sampling of recipes in this volume, from the all-important pastes to snacks, soups, vegetables, and desserts, showcases Thai food as it would be prepared and served throughout Thailand. We have tried to use chili peppers and spices authentically, but have toned down the heat in deference to the uninitiated Western palate (See *Panaeng Beef Curry*, page 54, for example). We suggest that you use chilis judiciously in any dish you are making for the first time; you can always increase the heat quotient, but once added to a dish, the power of a chili cannot be removed.

A fork and spoon are the only utensils used on a Thai table; the Thai people believe that the food should be so expertly cut in preparation that a knife will not be needed. This aesthetic, along with exquisitely carved fruits and vegetables for garnish, displays the delicate attributes of the Thai spirit and helps to explain why Thai cooking has become a celebrated, world-class cuisine. Its superb and unusual tastes and delicate complexities endure far beyond the close of any meal.

Evie Righter

Nam Prik Gaeng Keow Wan

Green Curry Paste

Although pastes and sauces are usually mere accompaniments to a dish, all Thais would agree that these four ~ green curry paste, red curry paste, panaeng curry paste, and Masaman curry paste ~ are quintessential components in flavoring. Other ingredients may add to the overall taste of a dish, but the paste is the keystone. Green curry paste is very hot, but it also has a refreshingly cool quality, a result of the amount of lemongrass. The heat of a chili pepper resides in the seeds; handle both fresh and dried chilis carefully. To temper the heat, make the paste with fewer chilis, then keep adding more until you have the fire power you desire.

½ teaspoon dried kaffir lime rind

3 garlic cloves, chopped

2 teaspoons minced fresh or frozen galangal

7 small fresh green chili peppers, stems removed & chopped

1 teaspoon shrimp paste

1 teaspoon salt

1 medium shallot, chopped

4 coriander roots

¼ teaspoon coriander seeds

¼ cup chopped lemongrass

1 to 2 tablespoons water

Soak lime rind in warm water to cover 10 to 15 minutes, or until just softened. Drain and discard water.

In a food grinder, process lime rind, garlic, galangal, chilis, shrimp paste, salt, shallot, coriander roots, coriander seeds, and lemongrass until smooth. Gradually add 1 to 2 tablespoons water to assist in the blending. The paste should be smooth but not wet. Store in an airtight container in the refrigerator 1 to 2 weeks, or freeze up to 6 months. Makes about ½ cup.

Nam Prik Gaeng Ped

Red Curry Paste

Vibrant in color, red curry paste has many of the same ingredients
as green curry paste, but in notably different amounts. It has
another salient difference: It relies upon dried red chilis ~ lots of them ~
for its knockout punch. Because chilis vary in size and flavor,
adjust the amount as you see fit. This unique culinary creation ~ hot,
garlicky, and bold ~ is a good paste for the heat of the tropics.

14 small dried red chili peppers

2 medium shallots, chopped

8 garlic cloves, chopped

2 tablespoons minced fresh or
frozen galangal

2 stalks lemongrass, thinly
sliced

1 teaspoon white peppercorns

1/2 teaspoon coriander seeds

2 coriander roots

1 1/2 teaspoons shrimp paste

1 to 2 tablespoons water

Soak chilis in water to cover about 1 hour, or until just softened. Drain and discard water.

In a food grinder, process chilis, shallots, garlic, galangal, lemongrass, peppercorns, coriander seeds, coriander roots, and shrimp paste until smooth. Gradually add 1 to 2 tablespoons water to assist in the blending. The paste should be smooth but not wet. Store in an airtight container in the refrigerator for 1 to 2 weeks, or freeze up to 6 months. Makes about 1/2 cup.

Nam Prik Panaeng

Panaeng Curry Paste

This is the paste that defines a Panaeng curry and, like the other Thai sauces, lends itself to advance preparation. This version is hot, but not overwhelmingly so, and achieves a very successful balance of the sweet, salty, and sour tastes that distinguish the cooking of Thailand.

12 small dried red chili peppers

2 stalks lemongrass, thinly sliced

2 large shallots, thinly sliced

4 garlic cloves, chopped

2 teaspoons coriander seeds

1 teaspoon salt

2 teaspoons minced fresh or frozen galangal

1 teaspoon shrimp paste

1 to 2 tablespoons water

Soak chilis in warm water to cover about 1 hour, or until just softened. Drain and discard water.

In a food grinder, process chilis, lemongrass, shallots, garlic, coriander seeds, salt, galangal, and shrimp paste until smooth. Gradually add 1 to 2 tablespoons water to assist in the blending. The paste should be smooth but not wet. Store in an airtight container in the refrigerator 1 to 2 weeks, or freeze up to 6 months. Makes about ⅔ cup.

Wieng Lakon festival near Lampang, in northern Thailand

Nam Prik Gaeng Masaman

Masaman Curry Paste

Masaman, which means Muslim, is the most popular Thai curry. Inherited from India, it is not surprising to find this richly flavored combination filled with the treasures of the spice routes ~ cardamom pods, cumin seeds, black pepper, and Indian bay leaves. This paste serves as a base for the sauce in Masaman Beef Curry (page 52) and can be used with both chicken and seafood. It is hot ~ deliciously so ~ and lovely in color.

1 tablespoon coriander seeds

½ teaspoon cumin seeds

8 whole cardamom pods

4 Indian bay leaves

20 small dried red chili peppers

6 garlic cloves, chopped

2 medium shallots, chopped

4 coriander roots, chopped

2 teaspoons minced fresh or frozen galangal

2 stalks lemongrass, thinly sliced

1½ teaspoons shrimp paste

1 teaspoon black peppercorns

1½ teaspoons salt

1 to 2 tablespoons water

In a medium skillet, combine coriander seeds, cumin seeds, cardamom pods, bay leaves, and chilis and cook over medium heat, shaking the skillet, about 1 minute. Remove the bay leaves and cardamom pods and reserve to use in Masaman Beef Curry. Continue to cook the spices 2 to 3 min-utes, or until chilis darken but do not turn black. Remove from heat.

In a food grinder, process garlic, shal-lots, coriander roots, galangal, and lemongrass for 10 seconds. Gradually add roasted spices (not including bay leaves and cardamom pods), shrimp paste, pep-

Masaman Beef Curry, page 52

percorns, and salt and process until smooth. Gradually add 1 to 2 tablespoons water to assist in the blending. The paste should be smooth but not wet. Store in an airtight container in the refrigerator 1 to 2 weeks, or freeze up to 6 months. Makes about ½ cup.

Nam Jim Satay

Satay Sauce

While some satay sauces use peanut butter as a base, this one authentically uses roasted peanuts and a hint of curry paste for hotness. Tamarind juice, coconut milk and cream, and other aromatic Thai and Indian seasonings add to its complex but mellow exoticness. When grinding the peanuts, be sure not to overprocess them or you will end up with peanut butter.

3 whole garlic cloves

12 thin slices fresh or frozen galangal

1 stalk lemongrass, chopped

¼ teaspoon black pepper

3 tablespoons chopped fresh mild red chili peppers

¼ teaspoon shrimp paste

2 tablespoons vegetable oil

½ cup coconut cream (p. 94)

2 tablespoons coconut milk (p. 94)

¾ cup shelled roasted unsalted peanuts, ground

2 tablespoons sugar

¼ teaspoon salt

½ cup water

1 tablespoon tamarind pulp soaked in 3 tablespoons warm water

1 tablespoon nam pla (fish sauce)

⅛ teaspoon ground coriander

⅛ teaspoon curry powder

2 teaspoons Panaeng or Masaman Curry Paste (p. 13 or 14)

In a food grinder, process garlic, galangal, lemongrass, pepper, chilis, and shrimp paste until smooth. In a skillet, heat oil over medium-high heat until hot but not smoking. Add garlic mixture and stir-fry 30 seconds, or until fragrant. Add ¼ cup

Elephants at work in the northern city of Chang Mai

coconut cream and coconut milk and bring to a boil. Add peanuts and cook 1 to 2 minutes, stirring constantly, until thickened. Add remaining coconut cream, sugar, salt, and water and bring to a boil. Reduce heat to low and cook, uncovered, stirring constantly, 10 minutes, or until slightly thickened.

Strain tamarind pulp, reserving juice. Add tamarind juice, *nam pla*, coriander, curry powder, and curry paste to the skillet and bring to a boil over medium heat. Simmer, uncovered, stirring constantly, 10 to 15 minutes, or until thickened. Store in an airtight container in the refrigerator for 3 to 4 days. Makes 2 cups.

Gai Satay

C h i c k e n   S a t a y

Thai satays are recognized the world over. These kebabs are exotic, flavorful, and easy to prepare. They can also be varied: Use 1¼ pounds boneless pork loin or flank steak, but be sure the slices are all the same thickness to ensure even cooking. For best results, let the skewered meat marinate overnight.

4 chicken breast halves, boned & skinned (about 1¼ pounds)

2 whole garlic cloves

8 coriander roots

2 medium shallots, chopped

1 tablespoon curry powder

½ teaspoon salt

1 teaspoon sugar

½ teaspoon ground coriander seeds

½ teaspoon turmeric

¼ cup nam pla *(fish sauce)*

2 tablespoons vegetable oil

½ teaspoon black pepper

6 tablespoons coconut cream (p. 94)

Satay Sauce (p. 16)

Cut chicken halves lengthwise into 3 even slices. Pound chicken with the back of a knife until ½ inch thick.

In a food grinder, process garlic, coriander roots, and shallots until smooth. In a shallow bowl, combine chicken, garlic mixture, curry powder, salt, sugar, coriander seeds, turmeric, *nam pla*, oil, pepper, and 4 tablespoons coconut cream. Cover with plastic wrap and refrigerate at least 1 hour, preferably overnight.

Soak twelve 12-inch bamboo skewers in cold water for at least 1 hour. Thread each slice of chicken down the center onto a

skewer, being careful not to tear meat or expose skewer.

Preheat grill or broiler. Brush skewered chicken with 1 tablespoon coconut cream and place on grill or broiler pan 4 inches from heat 5 to 6 minutes. Turn, brush with remaining tablespoon coconut cream, and grill 3 to 4 minutes, or until cooked through. Serve with Satay Sauce. Makes 12 skewers; 4 multi-course servings.

Taud Man Pla

F i s h   C a k e s *(picture p. 23)*

Thai cooks put the bounty of their waters to superb use. These fish cakes, made with cod filling, are accented by a judicious amount of red curry paste. Deep-frying adds texture, and a fresh cucumber condiment adds coolness and crunch.

1 small cucumber

2 tablespoons sugar

½ cup boiling water

2 small fresh red chili peppers, seeded & chopped

3 tablespoons white vinegar

½ teaspoon salt

1 medium shallot, finely chopped

1 pound cod or white fish fillets, skinned

2 tablespoons nam pla *(fish sauce)*

2 tablespoons Red Curry Paste (p. 11)

One ½-inch piece fresh or frozen galangal, finely chopped

1 egg

8 fresh kaffir lime leaves, center vein of each removed, finely shredded

¼ teaspoon white pepper

2 cups vegetable oil

Score cucumber, remove seeds, thinly slice, and place in bowl. Dissolve sugar in boiling water and pour over cucumber. Add chilis, vinegar, salt, and shallot and refrigerate until ready to use.

Check fish fillets for bones. Cut fish into 1-inch pieces. In a food processor, process fish for 10 seconds, or until finely chopped. Add *nam pla*, curry paste, galangal, egg, lime leaves, and pepper and

A fisherman on the Andaman Sea

process until just combined. Wet hands with water. Using ¼ cup of fish mixture at a time, form into 12 balls, then flatten into ¼-inch-thick patties.

In a wok, heat oil to 375°F. Fry fish cakes, 3 to 4 at a time, 5 minutes, or until golden brown, turning midway through cooking. Drain on several layers of paper towels. Serve with cucumber-chili mixture. Makes 12 small fish cakes; 6 multi-course servings.

Ma Ha

Galloping Horses

Ma means horse in both Chinese and Thai, but what galloping has to do with these delectable appetizers is not abundantly clear – unless it is to suggest how fast they disappear! Fresh pineapple slices serve as the base for a flavorful sweet pork and peanut mixture. Do not refrigerate these once assembled, as the pork fat will solidify and become less appetizing.

2 garlic cloves, chopped

2 coriander roots, chopped

½ teaspoon black pepper

½ teaspoon salt

2 tablespoons vegetable oil

6 ounces ground pork (about ¾ cup)

2 large shallots, thinly sliced

2 tablespoons palm sugar

1 tablespoon nam pla (fish sauce)

½ cup shelled roasted unsalted peanuts, ground

½ small ripe pineapple

Slivered fresh red chili peppers & coriander sprigs for garnish

In a food grinder, process garlic, coriander roots, pepper, and salt until smooth. Set aside.

In a wok, heat oil over medium-high heat until hot but not smoking. Add garlic paste and stir-fry 30 seconds, or until fragrant. Add pork and stir-fry 30 seconds. Add shallots and cook, stirring constantly, until pork is almost white. Add sugar and cook, stirring constantly, until just combined. Add *nam pla* and peanuts and reduce heat to low. Cook, uncovered, 6 to 8 minutes, stirring frequently, until slightly thickened. Drain mixture to remove excess oil and set aside to cool.

Remove rind and eyes of pineapple and

Galloping Horses & Fish Cakes, page 20

core it. Cut pineapple into bite-size, ¼-inch-thick slices. (You should have about 24 slices.) When pork mixture is cool, mound 2 teaspoons on each slice of pineapple. Garnish with chilis and coriander sprigs. Serve at room temperature. Makes 6 to 8 multi-course servings.

Khai Luk Koei

Son-in-Law Eggs

Once upon a time in Thailand, a son-in-law wanted to impress his mother-in-law, so he created these eggs. These deep-fried, hard-boiled eggs sauced with an almost saffron-colored combination are absolutely unique, wonderful to taste, and perfectly beautiful on a plate. Be careful when frying them. Use a splatter screen to avoid the hot oil that sputters up when the eggs are added, and a metal spatula and wooden chopsticks to turn them in the oil ~ they have a tendency to stick.

2 small dried red chili peppers

¼ cup tamarind pulp soaked in ½ cup warm water

1 cup vegetable oil

4 hard-boiled eggs, peeled

3 medium shallots, thinly sliced

¾ teaspoon salt

3 tablespoons palm sugar

½ teaspoon cornstarch dissolved in 2 teaspoons water

Shredded fresh red chili pepper & coriander sprigs for garnish

Soak dried chilis in warm water to cover until just softened. Drain and discard water. Finely shred chilis and set aside. Strain tamarind pulp, reserving juice.

In a small saucepan large enough to fit the eggs, heat oil over medium-high heat to 375°F. Carefully add eggs and fry 1 to 2 minutes, turning carefully, until golden brown. Remove with slotted spoon to paper towels to drain.

Remove all but 2 tablespoons oil from the pan. Add ⅔ of the shallots and stir-fry 1 to 2 minutes, or until crispy. Remove with slotted spoon to paper towels to

drain. Add chilis and stir-fry 30 seconds, or until crispy. Remove with slotted spoon to paper towels to drain. Remove all but 1 tablespoon oil from pan. Add remaining shallot and stir-fry 1 minute. Add tamarind juice and salt, and bring to a boil. Add sugar and cook, stirring constantly, until just combined. Add cornstarch mixture and cook 1 minute, or until slightly thickened.

Halve the eggs and place on a small platter. Sprinkle with fried shallots and chilis. Drizzle the sauce over eggs and garnish with fresh chili and coriander sprigs. Makes 4 multi-course servings.

Po Pia Taud

Spring Rolls

The crabmeat in this recipe can be replaced by ¼ pound ground pork.

½ cup crabmeat

1 package (1.7 ounces) dried
    bean thread noodles

4 garlic cloves, chopped

3 tablespoons chopped
    coriander root

2 ounces ground pork
    (about ¼ cup)

¼ pound shrimp, shelled,
    deveined, & finely chopped

½ cup sliced bamboo shoots,
    rinsed & chopped

½ cup chopped celery

¼ cup chopped scallions

1 cup bean sprouts

⅓ cup shredded carrots

1 egg

1 tablespoon nam pla (fish
    sauce)

¼ teaspoon white pepper

1 tablespoon plus 3¾ cups
    vegetable oil

10 spring roll wrappers

Remove any cartilage from crab and break into bite-size pieces. In a medium bowl, soak noodles in warm water to cover 10 to 15 minutes, or until just softened. Drain and discard water. Roughly chop noodles.

In a food processor, process garlic and coriander root until finely minced. Add pork and shrimp and process until just combined. Transfer to a large bowl. Add noodles, bamboo shoots, celery, scallions, bean sprouts, carrots, egg, *nam pla*, and pepper and toss gently until well combined.

In a wok, heat 1 tablespoon oil over medium-high heat until hot but not smoking. Add mixture and stir-fry 3 to 5 minutes, or until pork and shrimp are

cooked through, egg is set, and vegetables are just limp. Stir in crab. Transfer to a large bowl, cover with plastic wrap, and let cool.

To form spring rolls, place 1 wrapper on cutting board with tip facing you. Put $1/4$ cup mixture near the bottom tip, covering an area $3/4$ by 2 inches. Fold the tip facing you back over the mixture and roll the wrapper tightly, folding in the sides as you go. Place seam side down. Repeat with remaining wrappers and filling. If a wrapper does not seal, moisten tip with water.

In a wok, heat remaining oil over high heat to 375°F. Fry 3 to 4 spring rolls at a time, 2 to 3 minutes, or until golden brown. Remove with a slotted spoon to paper towels to drain. Makes 10 spring rolls; 5 multi-course servings.

Tom Kha Gai

Chicken and Galangal in Coconut Milk Soup

Soup is a favorite component of the Thai meal and can be broth-based and light or very rich and sweet, as is this coconut-milk-and-cream-based combination. The chilis here render the overall effect hot, but not searingly so. The whole kaffir lime leaves, if soft enough when cooked, are to be eaten; the chilis are definitely not.

4 cups coconut milk (p. 94)

2 stalks lemongrass, cut in 2-inch pieces & smashed

6 thin slices fresh or frozen galangal

1 pound chicken breast halves, boned & skinned

4 fresh kaffir lime leaves, center vein of each removed

6 small fresh red or green chili peppers, lightly smashed

½ cup coconut cream (p. 94)

2 tablespoons nam pla (fish sauce)

2 tablespoons lime juice

Coriander sprigs for garnish

In a medium saucepan, heat coconut milk over medium heat until gently simmering. Add lemongrass and galangal and simmer, uncovered, 5 minutes, or until fragrant.

Cut chicken into 1-inch cubes. Add to simmering coconut milk and bring to a boil over medium-high heat. Reduce heat to medium and cook, stirring frequently, 3 to 4 minutes, or until chicken is just firm. Stir in lime leaves, chilis, and coconut cream and cook over medium heat, 1 to 2 minutes, or until just heated through.

Spoon soup and 1½ teaspoons each of *nam pla* and lime juice into 4 soup bowls. Garnish with coriander sprigs. Makes 4 multi-course servings.

Gway Tio Neua Nam

Beef and Rice Flour Noodle Soup

Cinnamon and star anise enrich the aroma of this simple but substantial soup. Use fresh rice flour noodles, which contribute a creamy, soft texture and, to be typically Thai, a bottle of chilis in vinegar to accompany this dish.

1½ pounds beef shin, trimmed

2 teaspoons sugar, plus additional for serving

3 tablespoons vegetable oil

2 teaspoons cornstarch

6 cups homemade beef stock

10 black peppercorns, crushed

1 star anise

One 2-inch stick Thai cinnamon

2 coriander roots

½ teaspoon salt

3 garlic cloves, minced

1 pound fresh rice flour noodles, cut in ½-inch-wide strips

3 cups bean sprouts

1 to 2 tablespoons bottled chilis in vinegar

⅓ cup chopped coriander sprigs, for garnish

2 scallions, chopped, for garnish

Cut beef into 1-inch cubes.

In a medium bowl, combine the beef, sugar, 1 tablespoon oil, and cornstarch and set aside. In a large stockpot over high heat, bring stock to a boil. Add peppercorns, star anise, cinnamon stick, coriander roots, and salt. Add beef and boil 1 minute, skimming the foam that rises to the surface. Cover, reduce heat to low, and simmer 1½ to 2 hours, or until beef is tender when pierced with a knife. Remove to a plate and cover loosely with plastic wrap.

Strain broth into another pot, discard spices, and keep broth warm.

In a wok, heat remaining oil over high heat until hot but not smoking. Add garlic and stir-fry 2 to 3 minutes, or until golden brown. Remove to paper towels.

When the beef is cooked through, in a medium saucepan, bring 4 cups water to a boil. Add noodles and cook 30 seconds to 1 minute, or until just softened and heated through. Drain and discard water.

In a large saucepan of boiling water, blanch bean sprouts for 30 seconds. Drain thoroughly.

Divide the bean sprouts, broth, noodles, and beef among 6 soup bowls. Drizzle chilis in vinegar into each bowl and sprinkle with a pinch of sugar. Garnish with fried garlic, coriander, and scallions. Makes 6 multi-course servings.

Tom Yam Goong

Hot and Sour Shrimp Soup

You will need a rich, full-flavored chicken stock as a base for this refreshing soup. It must be crystal clear to allow the captivating coral-pink highlights of the shrimp to shine through. In Thailand, you would be using prawns, which are also available in some of the larger Asian food markets here. Whether you are adding shrimp or prawns, be careful not to overcook them. They cook to tenderness in a matter of minutes and can become tough if left to stand.

4 cups homemade chicken stock

1 tablespoon nam pla (fish sauce)

1 tablespoon bottled nam prik paow

2 stalks lemongrass, cut in 2-inch pieces & smashed

5 fresh kaffir lime leaves, center vein of each removed

One 2-inch piece fresh or frozen galangal

¾ pound medium shrimp, shelled & deveined

1 cup canned straw mushrooms, rinsed & drained

2 tablespoons lime juice

Coriander sprigs for garnish

In a medium saucepan over high heat, bring stock, *nam pla, nam prik paow,* lemongrass, lime leaves, and galangal to a boil. Reduce heat to low and simmer, covered, 10 minutes. Return mixture to a boil over high heat, add shrimp and mushrooms, and cook 2 to 3 minutes, or until the shrimp are orange and just firm. Stir in lime juice, garnish with coriander sprigs, and serve immediately. Makes 4 multicourse servings.

Khao Tom Pla

S e a f o o d   R i c e   S o u p

This healthful soup is served in Thailand for breakfast or as a snack.

Fish Stock:

1½ pounds fish bones

Shells from ½ pound medium
  shrimp (reserved from
  shrimp, next column)

2 whole garlic cloves

1 stalk celery

2 thin slices fresh or frozen
  galangal

½ teaspoon salt

½ teaspoon black peppercorns

2 coriander roots

4 cups water

½ pound squid, cleaned

½ pound red snapper fillets,
  with skin

12 mussels, scrubbed &
  debearded

1 cup jasmine rice, rinsed

¼ cup vegetable oil

3 garlic cloves, minced

3 thin slices fresh or frozen
  galangal

¼ teaspoon black pepper,
  freshly ground

½ pound medium shrimp,
  shelled & deveined

1½ teaspoons salt

2 tablespoons nam pla *(fish
  sauce)*

1 tablespoon chopped coriander
  sprigs, for garnish

1 scallion, finely chopped, for
  garnish

To make the Fish Stock, in a large stock-pot, combine all the stock ingredients with water. Cover and bring to a boil over high heat. Reduce heat to low, cover, and simmer 20 minutes. Let cool and strain.

Using a sharp knife, score squid ⅛ inch

deep to create an 'X' pattern. Cut fish into 1-inch pieces. Remove any bones. Wash mussels in several changes of cold water. Discard any that have opened. Drain.

In a large saucepan over high heat, bring 5 cups water to a boil. Add rice, return water to a boil, and cook, stirring frequently, 15 minutes, or until rice is wet, water is not visible, and mixture is thickened. Remove pan from heat and set aside.

In a wok, heat oil over medium heat until hot but not smoking. Add garlic and stir-fry 2 to 3 minutes, or until golden brown. Remove garlic and 3 tablespoons oil and set aside. Add squid, galangal, pepper, and shrimp and stir-fry 1 minute, or until squid turns white and curls. Add stock, mussels, and 1 teaspoon salt and, without stirring, bring to a boil over high heat. Add fish, remaining salt, and *nam pla* and boil until seafood is cooked and mussels have opened. Remove from heat and spoon into rice. Toss gently.

Divide soup among 6 bowls, discarding any closed mussels. Garnish with reserved garlic, garlic oil, coriander, and scallion. Makes 6 multi-course servings.

Pet Kao Lad

D u c k   w i t h   C h e s t n u t s

This two-step duck preparation is influenced not only by Chinese cooking techniques, but also by Chinese ingredients. It involves first steaming the bird, to render the meat moist and tender, then stir-frying it to bring out the aromas of sesame, soy, garlic, and scallion. The carved vegetable garnish and spark of hot red chili pepper, however, make this dish typically Thai.

1½ cups dried chestnuts

One 4½-pound duck, excess fat removed

2 teaspoons salt

3 tablespoons vegetable oil

2 garlic cloves, minced

2 teaspoons palm sugar

½ cup water

2 scallions, cut in 2-inch pieces

1 fresh red chili pepper, thinly sliced

1 tablespoon soy sauce

2 teaspoons sesame oil

Orange & radish "flowers" & fresh kaffir lime leaves for garnish

In a medium saucepan, place chestnuts in enough water to cover. Bring to a boil over high heat. Reduce heat to low, cover, and cook 20 to 30 minutes, or until tender when pierced with a knife. Drain, set aside, and cover loosely with plastic wrap.

Remove and discard duck tail and rinse duck in cold water. Rub cavity and skin lightly with 1 teaspoon salt. Place duck in large bamboo steamer and cover with lid.

In a large wok over high heat, bring water to a boil. Place steamer in wok and steam duck for 1 hour, or until juices run clear when duck is pierced with a knife. Monitor water in wok to make sure it does not evaporate and add more as necessary.

Remove duck and let cool. Debone breast and leg meat. Leave skin on and cut meat into ¼-inch-thick slices.

In a wok, heat oil over medium-high heat until hot but not smoking. Add garlic and stir-fry 30 seconds, or until fragrant. Add duck slices and remaining teaspoon salt and cook, stirring constantly, 2 to 3 minutes. Add chestnuts, sugar, and water and cook, stirring constantly, until heated through. Add scallions, chili, soy sauce, and sesame oil and cook, stirring constantly, 2 to 3 minutes, or until heated through. Transfer to a platter and garnish with orange and radish flowers and kaffir lime leaves. Makes 6 multi-course servings.

Gai Phad Saus Tua

Chicken in Spicy Peanut Sauce

Those who love Thai food know how successfully peanuts are used in this cuisine. Here, they again add their singular sweet appeal. Steamed rice is an essential accompaniment to counter the spiciness of this dish.

1 pound chicken breast halves and thighs, boned & skinned

½ cup skinless raw peanuts

¼ cup chopped ginger

5 garlic cloves, chopped

2 tablespoons Red Curry Paste (p. 11)

½ cup coconut cream (p. 94)

2 tablespoons vegetable oil

8 medium shallots, finely chopped

¼ teaspoon minced fresh red chili pepper

2 teaspoons sugar

1 tablespoon nam pla (fish sauce)

1 cup coconut milk (p. 94)

Fresh Thai basil sprigs for garnish

Cut chicken into 1-inch cubes and place in medium bowl.

In a medium skillet, roast peanuts over medium heat, shaking the skillet frequently, 5 to 10 minutes, or until golden brown. Remove from heat, let cool, then grind in food processor. (Do not overprocess or peanuts will turn to peanut butter.)

In food grinder, process ginger, garlic, and curry paste until just smooth. Add coconut cream and process until smooth. Pour mixture over chicken, stir until well combined, and cover. Refrigerate for 30 minutes.

In a wok, heat oil over medium heat until hot but not smoking. Add shallots

Kanaa Namman Hoi

Sautéed Oriental Broccoli with Oyster Sauce

In Thai cooking, vegetable dishes are often garnished with a little pork,
chicken, or shrimp to highlight the other flavors. Here the
shrimp garnish contributes a lustrous pink to the dark,
rich green of the Chinese broccoli. The broccoli can be prepared as
described, or can be cooked whole. To cook whole, trim the stalks by
½ inch and peel them. Then cut crosses, about 2 to 3 inches deep, at the
stem ends, to help them cook faster.

1½ pounds Chinese broccoli

2 tablespoons vegetable oil

2 garlic cloves, minced

½ pound medium shrimp,
   shelled & deveined

3 to 4 tablespoons oyster sauce

1 to 2 tablespoons water

Trim bottoms from broccoli stalks. Cut stalks on the diagonal into 2-inch pieces. Set stalk pieces and leafy portions aside separately.

In a wok, heat oil over medium high heat until hot but not smoking. Add garlic and stir-fry 30 seconds, or until fragrant. Add the shrimp and stir-fry 1 minute, or until orange. Push shrimp to the side of the wok, add broccoli stalks, and stir-fry 1 minute. Add the leafy portions and stir-fry 1 minute. Add oyster sauce and water, bring shrimp to the center of wok, and cook, stirring constantly, until well combined and the shrimp are cooked through. Makes 4 multi-course servings.

Tom Kati Pak Ruam

Mixed Vegetables in Coconut Milk

Coconut, along with its milk and cream, is an integral element in Thai cuisine. In Thailand, fresh coconut is sold, already shredded, in the markets, but shredded fresh coconut, the basis of coconut milk, is not so easily found in this country.

Some Thais like to add chopped fresh shrimp with the last addition of coconut milk ~ and vegetarians can prepare this without shrimp paste or the fresh shrimp. Serve with bottled *nam prik paow,* the typical spicy Thai condiment.

1½ cups water

8 small shallots, thinly sliced

1 teaspoon shrimp paste

1¼ cups coconut milk (p. 94)

1½ pounds assorted vegetables, such as: green beans, cut in 2-inch lengths; Thai eggplant, stem removed &

cut in 8 wedges; acorn squash, peeled, seeded, & cut into ¼-inch-thick slices

1 teaspoon sugar

½ teaspoon salt

Fresh Thai basil leaves for garnish

In a wok over high heat, bring water to a boil. Add shallots, shrimp paste, and ¼ cup coconut milk and bring to a boil. Add vegetables and bring to a boil. Add sugar and salt and reduce heat to medium. Simmer 3 to 4 minutes, stirring constantly, or until vegetables are just tender. Add remaining coconut milk and return to a boil, stirring constantly, 1 minute. Remove wok from heat. Serve vegetables in coconut milk sauce accompanied by *nam prik paow,* if desired, and garnish with basil leaves. Makes 4 to 6 multi-course servings.

Pad Tua Ngog

Stir-Fried Bean Sprouts and Chives

Fresh Chinese chives, called *gau choy*, are available in Asian food markets. They have a subtle onion flavor, unlike scallions or the chives American cooks are used to, and lend their aroma to the mild flavors of pork and bean sprouts. The lime condiment ~ twelve fresh chilis, garlic, a few seasonings, and fresh lime juice ~ renders this dish very hot, but not alarming.

1/2 pound boneless pork loin

1/4 pound Chinese chives

1 pound bean sprouts

3 tablespoons vegetable oil

1 garlic clove, minced

3 tablespoons oyster sauce

2 teaspoons nam pla *(fish sauce)*

1 1/2 teaspoons sugar

4 whole garlic cloves

6 small fresh red chili peppers, stems removed & chopped

6 small fresh green chili peppers, stems removed & chopped

1 teaspoon salt

Juice of 1 lime

Cut pork with grain into 2-inch-wide strips, then cut each strip against grain into ¼-inch-thick slices. Trim 1 inch off the bottom of a bunch of chives and 1½ inches off the chives themselves. Wash and cut chives into 1½-inch pieces. (You should have 1 cup chives.) Wash bean sprouts under cold water and drain thoroughly.

In a wok, heat oil over medium-high heat until hot but not smoking. Add minced garlic and stir-fry 1 minute, or until fragrant. Add pork and stir-fry 1 to 2 minutes, or until it just begins to turn white. Add 1 tablespoon oyster sauce and stir-fry 1 minute. Add bean sprouts and stir-fry 1 to 2 minutes, or until sprouts

A woman selling produce at the floating market in Damnoensaduak

begin to wilt. Add chives, remaining oyster sauce, *nam pla*, and ½ teaspoon sugar and stir-fry 1 to 2 minutes, or until chives have wilted, bean sprouts are just tender, and pork is cooked through.

With a mortar and pestle, pound whole garlic until mashed. Add remaining sugar, chilis, and salt and pound until mashed and well combined. Stir in lime juice. Serve bean sprout mixture with the lime condiment. Makes 4 to 6 multi-course servings.

Pad Ma Khea

Sautéed Eggplant

Here is a robust vegetarian dish that can be made even more flavorful
if the eggplant is first roasted over an open flame until the skin is charred,
then peeled and cut into bite-size pieces. Add the roasted eggplant
later in the recipe ~ after the oyster sauce. Three reminders: With twelve
fresh chilis, even small ones, this registers as hot on the scale of Thai
dishes; Oriental eggplants are the skinny, long ones, lavender in color; and
yellow bean sauce, a uniquely Thai ingredient, will have to be bought in an
Asian food market. There is no substitute for it.

6 Oriental eggplants (about
    2½ pounds)

12 small fresh green chili
    peppers

4 whole garlic cloves

10 coriander roots, chopped

½ small yellow onion, chopped

3 tablespoons vegetable oil

1 garlic clove, minced

30 fresh Thai basil leaves, plus
    additional for garnish

¼ cup yellow bean sauce

2 tablespoons plus ⅓ cup water

¼ cup oyster sauce

1 tablespoon finely shredded
    fresh red chili pepper

Chili pepper flowers for garnish

Cut eggplants on the diagonal into ¼-inch-thick slices and set aside.

In a food grinder, process green chilis, whole garlic, coriander roots, and onion until smooth.

In a wok, heat oil over medium-high heat until hot and beginning to smoke. Add minced garlic and stir-fry 20 seconds, or until fragrant. Add chili mixture and stir-fry 30 seconds, or until fragrant. Add

the eggplant and 10 of the basil leaves and cook, stirring constantly, 3 to 4 minutes. Add bean sauce and 2 tablespoons water and cook, stirring constantly, 1 to 2 minutes, or until well combined. Add oyster sauce, 1/3 cup water, and 10 more basil leaves. Cook, stirring constantly, 2 to 3 minutes, or until eggplant is cooked through. Add red chilis and remaining basil leaves and cook 1 minute. Garnish with basil leaves and chili flowers. Makes 6 multi-course servings.

Sangkaya Fak Thong

Coconut Milk Custard in Acorn Squash

Pumpkin, which is put to good use in the cooking of Thailand, would normally be used in this very popular dessert. In the United States, however, fresh pumpkins are seasonal and often uncompromising in size. Acorn squash, which is generally much more available, has been substituted.

The method of combining the eggs and sugar within plastic wrap instead of with a fork or whisk is to prevent the eggs from gaining any volume. Thai cooks use banana leaves, far more exotic and poetic, instead of plastic wrap.

2 medium acorn squash (each 1½ pounds)

4 large eggs

¼ cup palm sugar

1⅓ cups coconut milk (p. 94)

Shave off a thin piece from the bottom of each acorn squash, without making a hole, so that squash can stand upright, stem side up. Remove each stem by carefully cutting a circle around it about ¾ inch from the stem. Reserve cutout stems. Scrape out the seeds and pulp and discard.

Place eggs and sugar in a medium bowl. Cut a 4-inch square of plastic wrap and place in bowl. Using your fingers, rub eggs and sugar together through plastic wrap until well combined. Add coconut milk and continue "massaging" mixture until combined into a custard.

Carefully fill each squash with the custard, stopping ¾ inch from the top.

In a large wok over high heat, bring water to a boil. Place filled squash in a bamboo steamer with the stem tops at the side. Cover with bamboo lid and place steamer over boiling water. Steam over high heat 15 to 20 minutes, or until squash

is just tender and custard has set. Monitor water in wok to make sure it does not evaporate and add more if necessary. Let cool and refrigerate until ready to serve.

Cut squash into wedges. Makes 4 to 6 multi-course servings.

I-Tim Ma-Muang

Mango Ice Cream

After a succession of hotly spiced dishes in Thailand's tropical weather, you might finish a meal with fruit and this marvelous ice cream. You will need a ripe mango, which in Thailand, land of abundant, glorious fruit, is easy to come by. In this country, you will have to be the judge: The flesh of a ripe mango is fragrant and should give slightly to the touch. To ripen, leave the fruit out at room temperature for a day or two in a closed paper bag.

2 egg yolks

⅔ cup sugar

¾ cup milk

2 cups heavy cream

1 teaspoon vanilla extract

1 large ripe mango (about 1 pound), plus additional slices for garnish

In a heavy-bottomed medium saucepan, beat egg yolks and sugar together. Stir in milk until well combined. Cook over medium heat, stirring constantly with a whisk until thick enough to coat the back of a spoon, about 10 minutes. Remove pan from heat, cover, and let cool. Stir in heavy cream and vanilla until well combined. Cover and refrigerate until cold.

Peel and cut mango. Remove all flesh and discard seed. In a food processor, process mango flesh until slightly chunky. Stir mango into cold custard. Turn mixture into an ice cream maker and freeze according to the manufacturer's directions. Garnish scoops of ice cream with mango slices. Makes 4 to 6 multi-course servings.

Khao Neow Ma-Muang

Sticky Rice with Mango

The renowned combination of two of Thailand's most popular ingredients ~ coconut milk and rice ~ with fresh mango is a finale as soothing as it is pretty. Incidentally, the salt brings out the sweetness in the rice and prevents the coconut cream from souring in hot weather. This dessert is best served at room temperature.

1 cup sweet rice

1 cup coconut milk (p. 94)

⅓ cup plus 2 tablespoons sugar

¾ teaspoon salt

¼ cup coconut cream (p. 94)

1 ripe mango (about 1 pound)

Soak, rinse, and steam 1 cup sweet rice as directed on page 67.

In a small saucepan over medium heat, combine coconut milk, ⅓ cup sugar, and ½ teaspoon salt and cook, stirring constantly, 3 to 4 minutes, or until sugar is just dissolved. Pour ¼ cup over warm rice and toss gently until just combined. Pour remaining liquid over rice and toss gently until well combined. Cover and set aside 30 minutes.

In a small saucepan over medium heat, bring remaining sugar, salt, and coconut cream to a boil. Cook, uncovered, stirring frequently, 5 to 8 minutes, or until thickened.

Mound rice on an oval-shaped platter and drizzle with coconut cream mixture. Peel, halve, and cut mango into ½-inch-thick slices. Place next to rice on platter. Makes 4 multi-course servings.

Thai Basil: The leaves of this fresh herb resemble immature Italian basil, but are less sweet in flavor and more acidic in aroma. Don't confuse it with the hot (called holy basil) or reddish purple varieties, which are generally more difficult to find. Both the leaves and sprigs of Thai basil are used for garnishes. Store in a plastic bag in the refrigerator.

Fresh Chili Peppers: Called bird chilis, these typically hot Thai peppers, green or red in color, are about an inch long and tapered, and frequently come packaged in plastic bags in the markets. Do not be fooled by their size; they may be diminutive, but they pack a powerful punch. Wear rubber gloves when handling them and remember that their hotness resides in their seeds. If not available, substitute another hot fresh chili pepper, such as a serrano. Store, sealed in a plastic bag, in the refrigerator. Dried chili peppers are simply dried bird chilis, and should also be handled very carefully. Store in an airtight plastic bag.

Coriander Root: Coriander root is employed by Thai cooks more often than the leaves, which are usually used to garnish dishes. Wash, remove, and discard the stringy part of the root. Trim the remaining root up to the stem. If not using immediately, freeze in an airtight plastic bag. Keep stems and leaves wrapped in a damp paper towel in a plastic bag in the refrigerator.

***Nam Pla* (fish sauce):** Amber colored and clear, *nam pla* imparts a unique saltiness to a dish. Fish sauce is available in bottles in many different sizes and brands. Generally, the more expensive the brand, the more refined the flavor. Store, covered tightly, in the refrigerator.

Galangal: This relative of fresh ginger has a taste somewhere between ginger and pepper. You will find fresh or frozen galangal, which is also spelled galanga or galingale, with the herbs and vegetables in an Asian food market. It looks like ginger, with a stem and light-brown peel. Freeze galangal in airtight plastic bags. Do not try to substitute galangal powder, a pulverized dried variety of fresh galangal; the two are not interchangeable.

Pickled Garlic: Also called preserved garlic, this is a simple combination of peeled, whole heads of garlic, sugar, vinegar, and salt. It is not interchangeable with the fresh variety. Store in the refrigerator.

Kaffir Lime Leaves: Kaffir limes have a knobby texture and a vibrant green color and their leaves are particularly aromatic and edible. First devein them by folding each leaf in half, then peeling off the vein, starting with the stem. Store in a plastic bag in the refrigerator.

Lemongrass: Lemongrass, as its name suggests, lends a lemony taste to sauces, soup bases, or stir-fry combinations. Always remove the outer, reed-like stiff leaves and trim the end by about $1/2$ inch and the top of each stalk by 2 to 3 inches. Pound the thicker end of the stalk with the handle of a large kitchen knife to release the maximum amount of flavor. Lemongrass powder is not a substitute for the refreshing taste of the fresh variety. Store in plastic bags in the refrigerator.

Noodles: Dried rice noodles and bean threads, made from mung bean flour, lend a distinctive texture to a recipe. Different brands of rice noodles fry up differently. You may have to experiment to find the brand that provides the crispiest results. Dried noodles are available in packages.

Palm Sugar: With a light brown color and sticky texture, palm sugar lends a deep, rich sweetness to other ingredients with which it is combined. Store palm sugar in the refrigerator. If unavailable, light brown sugar or coconut sugar can be substituted.

Pickled Radish: This ingredient, which is also called "sweeten radish," is mustard-colored and has a sweet, vinegary aroma. It is available in Asian food markets, and usually comes in colorful plastic bags. Store in an airtight bag in the refrigerator.

Rice: Simply, rice is Thailand's most important dish, whether plain, with coconut milk, in soups, or in desserts. Jasmine rice (see page 66), a long-grain variety, is much favored and, although particularly fragrant when uncooked, becomes even more so when boiled. Sweet rice, which requires a completely different cooking technique from jasmine rice, is the base for the classic Thai dish Sticky Rice (page 67).

Dried Shrimp: Dried shrimp add texture

and a salty flavor to a recipe such as Pad Thai (see page 68). Available in plastic packages, they should be kept at room temperature.

Shrimp Paste: Shrimp paste is grayish-brown in color and strong in flavor and smell. Available in small, pillbox jars, shrimp paste contributes saltiness to a recipe. Store in the refrigerator.

Tamarind Pulp: The strained juice from tamarind pulp lends its remarkable sourness, assertiveness, and beautiful color to many dishes. The pulp is dark red-orange and has a pliable texture much like moist brown sugar. It must first be soaked in warm water, then strained in order to extract the juice; this step is usually repeated before the pulp is discarded. It can be found in Asian food markets and usually comes in a rectangle, clear plastic package. Store, tightly sealed in plastic wrap, in the refrigerator.

Spiced Tofu: Tofu is bean curd. Spiced tofu is curd that is cinnamony and licorice in flavor, with a reddish color and charac-teristic texture ~ chewy and resistant to the bite ~ very unlike regular bean curd. There is no substitute for what spiced tofu contributes in both flavor and texture to a dish. Look for it in packages of cakes in the refrigerated sections of Asian food markets. Store, covered, in the refrigerator.

Yellow Bean Sauce: Made from yellow beans, similar in shape and color to peanuts, this sauce lends a fullness and slight texture to any dish. It can be found in glass bottles in Asian food markets. Store in the refrigerator.

Preparing Fresh Coconut Milk and Cream

In curries and those recipes where the final taste is not so dependent upon the singular sweetness of fresh milk, canned coconut milk can be substituted. We recommend Chaokoh brand coconut milk, which comes in 13.5-ounce cans. In many recipes, however, there is simply no substitute for fresh-made coconut milk. The following steps will help you to prepare it at home.

1. Carefully puncture the 3 eyes at the top of a medium-size coconut with an ice pick, let the coconut water drain out, and discard. Bake the coconut for 20 to 30 minutes in a 375°F oven, or until it just cracks. Gently hit the coconut with a hammer to open. Use a blunt knife wedged between shell and flesh to carefully separate the two.

2. Dice the coconut flesh into ¼-inch pieces. In a food processor, process the coconut pieces until finely puréed, fluffy, and moist. Gradually add hot water to assist in the blending.

3. Add enough hot water to equal the amount of diced coconut and mix well. (For example, if you began with 2 cups diced flesh, and you have already added ⅔ cup water, you would now add an additional 1⅓ cups water to the puréed coconut.) Line a strainer with cheesecloth and pour the coconut mixture into it, letting it drain into a bowl. Squeeze the coconut mixture until dry. The resulting liquid will separate upon sitting: the top layer is cream; the bottom, milk. The cream and milk will only keep for 24 hours, so refrigerate immediately. Makes about ⅔ cup cream and 1⅓ cups milk.

A Word About Stir-Frying in Thai Cooking

As understood in Chinese cooking, stir-frying implies constantly tossing the ingredients in a wok or another ideally round-bottomed, slope-sided pan to encourage quick cooking for the maximum retention of texture and flavor. Thai cooking also stir-fries the seasonings ~ the garlic, onions, and galangal ~ in the Chinese manner. But after adding the other ingredients, which usually includes a certain amount of liquid, cook-stir rather than toss the mixture. In so doing, you do not break up the ingredients and alter the texture ~ a very important attribute of any well-prepared Thai dish.

WEIGHTS

OUNCES AND POUNDS   METRICS

¼ ounce ------------7 grams
⅓ ounce ------------10 grams
½ ounce ------------14 grams
1 ounce ------------28 grams
1¾ ounces ----------50 grams
2 ounces -----------57 grams
2⅔ ounces ----------75 grams
3 ounces -----------85 grams
3½ ounces ----------100 grams
4 ounces (¼ pound) ---114 grams
6 ounces -----------170 grams
8 ounces (½ pound) ---227 grams
9 ounces -----------250 grams
16 ounces (1 pound) --464 grams
1.1 pounds ---------500 grams
2.2 pounds ---------1,000 grams
(1 kilogram)

TEMPERATURES

°F (FAHRENHEIT)   °C (CENTIGRADE OR CELSIUS)

32 (water freezes) -------------0
108-110 (warm) --------------42-43
140 ------------------------60
203 (water simmers) ----------95
212 (water boils)-------------100
225 (very slow oven)----------107.2
245 ------------------------120
266 ------------------------130
300 (slow oven) -------------149
350 (moderate oven)----------177
375 ------------------------191
400 (hot oven) --------------205
425 ------------------------218
450 ------------------------232
500 (very hot oven) ----------260

LIQUID MEASURES

tsp.: teaspoon
Tbs.: tablespoon

SPOONS AND CUPS (8 ounces=1 cup)   METRIC EQUIVALENTS

1 tsp. ------------5 milliliters
(5 grams)
2 tsp. ------------10 milliliters
(10 grams)
3 tsp. (1 Tbs.) -----15 milliliters
(15 grams)
3⅓ Tbs. ----------½ deciliter
(50 milliliters)
¼ cup ------------59 milliliters
⅓ cup ------------1 deciliter less 1⅓ Tbs.

SPOONS AND CUPS   METRIC EQUIVALENTS

⅓ cup + 1 Tbs. ------1 deciliter
(100 milliliters)
1 cup ------------¼ liter less 1¼ Tbs.
1 cup + 1¼ Tbs. ----¼ liter
2 cups -----------½ liter less 2½ Tbs.
2 cups + 2½ Tbs. ---½ liter
4 cups -----------1 liter less 1 deciliter
4⅓ cups ----------1 liter
(1,000 milliliters)

INDEX